The Love Song of J. Robert Oppenheimer

by
CARSON KREITZER

Dramatic Publishing
Woodstock, Illinois • England • Australia • New Zealand

*** NOTICE ***

"Do I dare disturb the universe?"
  — *T.S. Eliot, The Love Song of J. Alfred Prufrock*

IMPORTANT BILLING AND CREDIT REQUIREMENTS

All producers of the Play *must* give credit to the Author of the Play in all programs distributed in connection with performances of the Play and in all instances in which the title of the Play appears for purposes of advertising, publicizing or otherwise exploiting the Play and/or a production. The name of the Author *must* also appear on a separate line, on which no other name appears, immediately following the title, and *must* appear in size of type not less than fifty percent (50%) the size of the title type. Biographical information on the Author, if included in the playbook, may be used in all programs. *In all programs this notice must appear:*

"Produced by special arrangement with
THE DRAMATIC PUBLISHING COMPANY of Woodstock, Illinois"

All producers of the Play must include the following acknowledgments on the title page of all programs distributed in connection with performances of the Play and on all advertising and promotional materials:

"Originally developed and presented by Frank Theatre, Minneapolis, Minnesota, Artistic Director, Wendy Knox."

"Originally produced by Cincinnati Playhouse in the Park, Edward Stern, Producing Artistic Director, Buzz Ward, Executive Director."

The Love Song of J. Robert Oppenheimer world premiered at the Cincinnati Playhouse in the Park (Ed Stern, Producing Artistic Director; Buzz Ward, Executive Director), March 22, 2003. It was directed by Mark Wing-Davey; the set design was by Douglas Stein; the costume design was by Catherine Zuber; the lighting design was by David Weiner; the sound design was by Marc Gwinn; the video design was by Rupert Bohle; the dramaturg was Kathleen Tobin; and the production stage manager was Jennifer Morrow. The cast was as follows:

J. Robert Oppenheimer . . . . Curzon Dobel
Lilith . . . . Judith Hawking
Young Scientist / Strauss, etc. . . . . Jason Bowcutt
Rabi / J .Edgar Hoover, etc. . . . . Michael Pemberton
Teller / Lansdale, etc. . . . . Steven Rattazzi
Kitty Oppenheimer . . . . Blaire Chandler
Jean Tatlock / Nurse / Mother, etc.. . . . . . Carolyn Baeumler

The Love Song of J. Robert Oppenheimer was commissioned with public funds from the Individual Artists Program of the New York State Council on the Arts, and written during a Jerome Fellowship at the Playwrights Center in Minneapolis.

The Love Song of J. Robert Oppenheimer was originally developed and presented by Frank Theatre, Minneapolis, Minnesota (Artistic Director Wendy Knox), February 6, 2003, as part of the Playwrights' Center's NewStage Directions program. It was directed by Wendy Knox; the set design was by John Francis Bueche; the costume design was by Kathy Kohl; the lighting design was by Michael P. Kittel; the sound design was by Reid Rejsa; the dramaturgs were Kathleen Tobin and Beth Cleary, and the production stage manager was Spencer Putney. The cast was as follows:

J. Robert Oppenheimer . . . . Phil Kilbourne
Lilith . . . . Maria Asp
Young Scientist / Strauss, etc. . . . . Patrick Bailey
Rabi / J.Edgar Hoover, etc. . . . . Tom Sherohman
Teller / Lansdale, etc. . . . . John Riedlinger
Kitty Oppenheimer. . . . . Annie Enneking
Jean Tatlock / Nurse / Mother, etc. . . . Gwendolyn Schwinke

The Love Song of J. Robert Oppenheimer

A Play in Two Acts
For 4m., 3w., with doubling.
May be expanded to 7 or more m., 5w.

CHARACTERS:

J. ROBERT OPPENHEIMER . . . . eminent physicist,
possible Communist

LILITH . . . . pre-Biblical demon, the first woman

KITTY OPPENHEIMER. . . . . wife

JEAN TATLOCK . . . . mistress
also MOTHER / CENSOR / REPORTER / NURSE

SCIENTIST ONE / RABI
also GROVES / SECURITY ONE / HOOVER

SCIENTIST TWO / TELLER
also VOICEOVER / LANSDALE / SECURITY TWO

SCIENTIST THREE / YOUNG SCIENTIST
also SOLDIER / BRITISH ENVOY / STRAUSS

NOTE: Lilith lives in the walls and ceiling, crawling up and across chain-link fence, perching, seething, lunging, curling up to sleep, but never touching the floor. She is only visible to Oppenheimer.

Action is continuous: The scene titles are for reader/actor orientation, and should not be felt by an audience, except in tone shift or light change.

LILITH: "Adam and Lilith never found peace together; for when he wished to lie with her, she took offense at the recumbent position he demanded. 'Why must I lie beneath you?' she asked. 'I also was made from dust, and am therefore your equal.' Because Adam tried to compel her obedience by force, Lilith, in a rage, uttered the magic name of God, rose into the air and left him."

— *Robert Graves and Raphael Patai,*
"Hebrew Mythology"

NOTES ON THE TEXT:

Passage from the Bhagavad-Gita translated by Barbara Stoller Miller.
T.S. Eliot misquote in the final scene is intentional.

PLAYWRIGHT'S NOTES:

Based on the productions I've seen, Act I should run one hour, Act II fifty minutes. This has been pretty consistent. Lilith is scarier if she's somehow damaged, not all-powerful. She's also sexier. For Jean's suicide, please have her dressed not in a slip, but in regular street clothes. This is not "find me dead and beautiful" but something much more deliberate and frightening. (The glamorous Jean in a slip in the courtroom is Oppie's memory of her; the one who commits suicide is the real woman.) Take care of the comedy, the scientists' occasional vaudeville, Oppie's twinkle in the eye. The pathos will take care of itself.

ACT I

(A faint Los Alamos desert dawn. OPPIE appears. He addresses the audience as though it were his clearance board.)

OPPIE. *And how should I presume?*

And how should I begin?

You have my file before you.

I trust this board will take into account not only certain political associations of an impassioned youth, but our needs as a country, and what I can do toward the task at hand. Certainly, I have associations with various communists, my wife and my brother to name two, and I have supported various causes and been a member of nearly every communist front group on the West Coast, but I have never engaged in anything even resembling subversive activities.

LILITH *(shadowing him).* ssssssubversssive

OPPIE. I am not ashamed of these political leanings. Only that they came rather late in life for me. They are a young man's politics. I had managed to remain shockingly ignorant of…the world and its ways. I read no newspapers, never had a radio. *(Smiles.)* I didn't hear about the stock-market crash until a friend told me, six months after.

But events conspired to pull me out of this…life of pure scholarship.
I had relatives in Germany.

I met a woman, to whom I was engaged for a time,

(JEAN appears, shadowy.)

who introduced me to various worthy causes including Spanish relief and the organization of migrant farm workers at home. I contributed sums of money because I could; I never considered joining the Communist Party because I prefer to do all of my thinking for myself.

I assure you, all this is firmly in my past. Now, in time of war, I only seek to serve my country in the way I best can. As the head of the laboratory currently being built on the spot I suggested for it, Los Alamos. Beautiful part of the country.
Desolate.

Empty.

The site, I have named
Trinity.
VOICEOVER *(whispered)*. What's a Jew doing naming it Trinity?
OPPIE. Batter my heart, three-person'd God
VOICEOVER. What?
OPPIE. It's Donne.
YOUNG SCIENTIST. Oppie?

OPPIE. What?

YOUNG SCIENTIST. It's done.

VOICEOVER. 14 July. Gadget complete. Should we have the chaplain here?

SCIENTIST ONE (RABI). Place your bets, gentlemen. Will we ignite the atmosphere and blow up the world? Or just the state of New Mexico?

SCIENTIST TWO (TELLER). It's not going to ignite the atmosphere! My calculations prove—

SCIENTIST THREE (YOUNG). How do you plan to collect?

VOICEOVER. Seven.

Six.

Five.

Four.

(The opening bars of the "Nutcracker Suite" are heard over the final numbers.)

Three

Two

One

(Flash of light. A tremendous explosion.)

YOUNG SCIENTIST. Is it the end of the world?

OPPIE. Maybe.

(LILITH laughs. She appears, teeth first, like the Cheshire Cat.)

That was the first time I saw your face.

LILITH. You must admit.
    It would have been funny.
OPPIE. What?
LILITH. If you had
    ignited the atmosphere.
    Consumed the world in a fiery ball.
OPPIE *(smiles)*. We were a little bit afraid.
LILITH. shows what you know.
OPPIE. Yes.
    We should have been much more so.

(LILITH makes a clicking noise like a lizard.)

An apple falls and hits a man on the head.
Thus begins Newtonian Physics. Which begat Theoretical Physics.
A discipline that ends, with great violence, July 16, 1945. Trinity.

I think this story is a metaphor. And it is knowledge which strikes Sir Isaac on the head.

The Apple of course its time-honored stand-in since Eve, the first woman, plucked one from the Tree of Knowledge. And that first sweet bite led to enlightenment. Banishment from the Garden. And eventual death.
LILITH. Sssssssssshhhheeee wass not the firsst.
OPPIE *(smiles)*. The early Hebrew tradition holds that there was another woman, before Eve. Made from earth, like Adam. Lilith.
LILITH. Lilit. Lillitû.* Lamashtû. Astarté. Ardat-lili
OPPIE *(overlaps)*. *But she would not behave.

LILITH. I dared disturb the Universe. God revoked my ssecurity clearance.

OPPIE. So God cast her out.

LILITH. I left.

OPPIE. Made a new one. Eve.

LILITH. From whom all you miserable creatures are descended.

And now here you are again.

A bunch of Jews in the desert.

Arguing esoteric points.

SCIENTIST ONE. You see, it is written

SCIENTIST TWO. It is easier for a camel to pass through the eye of a needle

SCIENTIST THREE. Than to ignite the earth's atmosphere. *(Beat.)*

SCIENTIST TWO *(concerned).*

Or a very thick piece of yarn.

Through the eye of a needle.

LILITH. What leads a kind man. A gentle man. A scholar. To make the biggest explosion the world has ever seen?

OPPIE. I had a...continuing, smoldering fury about the treatment of Jews in Germany.

LILITH. Ssmoldering.

20th CENTURY

(Sound of a train. OPPIE and GROVES in a train compartment.)

OPPIE *(smiling)*. Let us go then, you and I. The General and the Scientist. Still within the speed of the 20th Century…

GROVES. Strange name for a train, I always thought.

OPPIE. Hurtling toward an uncertain destination

GROVES. New York City. Though now that you mention it, I would call that an uncertain destination. *(Beat. He tries to figure out if this is the joke OPPIE was making.)* You understand, Dr. Oppenheimer, security is our number-one priority.

OPPIE. I thought getting the thing built was your priority.

GROVES. Well, yes, of course—

OPPIE. Then you've got to change the way things are being run. You can't just compartmentalize these people, have them toiling away in ignorance. Scientific discovery is built upon the free flow of ideas. You never know where the winning notion is going to come from. Sometimes the most unlikely of sources.

GROVES. Dr. Oppenheimer, we simply can't have this top-secret information being discussed out in the open—

OPPIE. YES YOU CAN— If. Instead of isolating each man. Isolate us all. The entire laboratory is top secret. But within this hermetic seal—no secrets. Everyone is working on the same problem. Give me thirty scientists, with complete freedom of discussion, and we can make this thing for you.

GROVES. We can't tell them anything about the project until they've agreed to work on it. Do you think you can recruit under those circumstances?

OPPIE. Yes. I believe I can.

LILITH. cocky bastard, aren'tcha?

OPPIE. Just practical.

Report to a post office box in New Mexico. Disappear.
And I got them.
Armed with nothing but the ever-growing list of lumi-
naries in attendance.

Fermi

Bethe

all our brightest graduate students

eventually the thing had a gravitational pull of its own.

LILITH. Creating a new star system?

OPPIE. No. Just…a world.

LILITH. A world powered by fury.

OPPIE. Our own world.

LILITH. The fury of the small.

OPPIE. A world of pure discovery.

LILITH. The fury of the cast-out.

(RABI and OPPIE, walking the perimeter fence at Los Alamos.)

RABI. I suppose this is all part of a rich historical tradition.

OPPIE. This, Isador?

RABI. At very regular intervals, there's a panic, and Jews
are accused of poisoning the wells. *(OPPIE nods.)*
Once a century, like clockwork.

OPPIE. I did not think it would happen in this one.

RABI. Chosen People, huh?

OPPIE. So they say.

LILITH. Chosen for the Pogrom. To bake your bread on
your very back as you leave one not a home for another
not a home.

You know what God does to his Favorites.

He does a Job on them.

oppie oppie oppie.

I could see this coming a century away.

OPPIE *(to LILITH)*. It's almost funny. In the German university system, all the Jews were forced into Theoretical Physics. The unfashionable end of the University. Less prestige, less pay. Now the greatest minds in the world are coming to us, refugees. Thoughts *smoking* out of their heads.

RABI. Those Nazis have signed their own death warrant.

(LILITH purrs.)

If we can just make the damn thing work.
Before they do.

(A SOLDIER approaches RABI.)

SOLDIER. Dr. Rabbi?
RABI. Rabi!

(Out.)

MOTHER'S HANDS

OPPIE. Lying awake at night, I think of…many things. Mostly the critical mass of fissionable material. The critical mass of scientists. Fissionable minds. Will we be able to translate Theory into Practice? In time—?

Sometimes I remember

my mother's hands
smoothing down my hair.
With the soft kidskin gloves she always wore. To cover
a...defect in her right hand. It was not fully formed.
Missing three fingers.
We never discussed it. It just...was.
Soft gloves touching my face. smoothing down my hair.
Sending me off to Dr. Adler's School for Ethical Cul-
ture. *(Smiles.)*

Ethical...Culture.
How young we all were.
To believe in such...possibilities.

(MOTHER appears. Takes off a large, broad-brimmed picture hat. Takes off one glove. Is about to take off the other. OPPIE turns to see her. She disappears.)

Once Dr. Adler brought a geologist in to speak to my
form. And this man brought with him a great iron contraption, much like a large ice chipper, and a box of un-
assuming-looking round brown rocks, only slightly
larger than a fist.
He rested one carefully in the contraption, brought the
handle down with a sharp CRACK, and there lay the geode, in two halves, inner cavern of crystals sparkling in
the first light it had ever seen.
I...laughed aloud. With the shock of it. The truth of it.
And I knew. I had got to look harder. To *know* what was
inside things.
Mineralogy was my first love.
It set me on a rather direct path...to here.

Los Alamos.
Where they question my associations. Read my mail.
Listen to every phone call. Listen at the keyhole till I
think I will go mad.

KITTY AND THE SECURITY MAN

*(The Oppenheimer home, Los Alamos. KITTY keeps a
man on the doorstep.)*

KITTY. I suppose I have to ask you in.
LANSDALE. Well, I don't think you want to leave me
   standing on your doorstep—
KITTY. ah but I do.
LANSDALE. Ahem. I have quite a few questions to ask
   you, actually. About your husband.
KITTY *(smiling)*. Which one?
LANSDALE. Well, now that you bring that up, all of
   them.
KITTY. In that case I suppose I have to ask you in.

*(She disappears. LANSDALE looks puzzled for a mo-
ment. There is the sound of a cocktail shaker. He follows
after her, gingerly.)*

LANSDALE. Uh, thank you for taking the time, Mrs.
   Oppenheimer—
KITTY *(reappearing)*. Martini?
LANSDALE. All right.
   Not the type to serve tea, then?
KITTY. I suppose it was your remarkable powers of obser-
   vation that landed you this security job.

LANSDALE. Touché.

KITTY. Gesundheit. *(She drinks more than a little of her martini.)* You won't find anything against my husband.

LANSDALE. Mrs. Oppenheimer, there is no need to be so adversarial. We're not out to "get" your husband.

KITTY *(smiling)*. Oh, please, Mr.—

LANSDALE. Colonel. Lansdale.

KITTY. Don't lie to me in my own home. *(Beat.)* Oh, I'm sorry, I suppose this is government housing. In that case, you can say anything you please.

LANSDALE. We just need to be as thorough as possible, on a project of this nature. You understand.

KITTY. Very well.

LANSDALE. Perhaps we should start with your first husband.

KITTY *(finishes her martini)*. Why not. I did. *(Laughs. Refills her drink from the shaker.)* More martini, Colonel? I made a batch.

LANSDALE. Uh, in a minute. About your first husband—

KITTY. Joe.

LANSDALE. Joe Dallet.

KITTY. sweet man.

LANSDALE. He was—

KITTY. A Communist. Yes. And he's dead. Died fighting the fascists in Spain. Nothing to be ashamed of. I left him because I couldn't take the poverty. That, perhaps, is something to be ashamed of. My second husband was a mistake. And Robert—Robert is the man I will spend my life beside. Even if it means coming here and living in a god-damned packing crate being grilled by junior J. Edgar Hoovers no offense meant I hope none taken more martini? *(He nods.)*

Robert will make you your thing. To stop Hitler.
You need him for that.

LANSDALE. He will be instrumental in the program, certainly, but there are many scientists—

KITTY. You need him for that.

You will poke and prod and write up your little reports saying his wife's a communist and she was married to a dead communist and he believed in subversive ideas like people getting paid a decent wage and having enough to eat but it will all come to nothing because you need him to make this thing work.

But what will you do afterward? That's what I want to know.

What will you do when you don't need him anymore.

LANSDALE *(laughing uncomfortably).* Say, I think I'm supposed to be asking the questions around here.

So your second husband, you say, was not a communist.

KITTY. No, he was a doctor. And a bore. And not a communist. *(Beat.)* Do you know why I am answering your questions? And entertaining you in my home with anything like a modicum of propriety? Do you know why?

LANSDALE. Because you love him.

KITTY *(surprised).* Yes.

LANSDALE. I have learned something about human nature. Doing this job.

KITTY. I'm impressed. *(Sound of a door opening.)* Hello, darling. How was the office?

OPPIE *(offstage).* Terrible. I had to fire my secretary.
She misplaced our October cravat order, so we'll never get the merchandise to Gimbels in time for Christmas.

KITTY *(to LANSDALE)*. You see? He tells me nothing. Your Atomic Secrets are safe.

OPPPIE. It's a tremendous blow to the Men's Neckwear campaign.

LANSDALE. That's not code?

KITTY *(bursts out laughing)*. A joke, Colonel. Not code.

OPPIE. I think the boss may fire me.

You and the children will be destitute.

KITTY. We're already destitute.

OPPIE *(entering)*. How can you say that? We've got a bathtub.

Oh, hello Colonel.

LANSDALE. Dr. Oppenheimer.

(Could it be a standoff? No, OPPIE de-fuses.)

OPPIE. I trust Kitty has made you feel welcome?

KITTY. Actually, I think I make him a bit nervous.

Don't know why. I'm the one who's been getting the third degree.

OPPIE. The Colonel is just doing his job, my dear. To ensure the safety of the project.

KITTY. Funny kind of a job, if you ask me.

OPPIE. It's a funny kind of a time. But we all do what we can.

LILITH. We all do what we can? What a pious little choirboy.

OPPIE *(to LILITH)*. It's got to work. I've got to make it work.

LILITH. Why do you stand for this continual invasion?

OPPIE. The alternative is unthinkable.

As many things are unthinkable. Now.

(They are alone.)

It's so quiet here. The desert seems to...absorb all sound.
makes the mind spin. Until it lands.
on...
my parents' silverware.

If we did not believe, why the two sets of silverware?
One for the milk. One for the meat.
Patterns.
These are the stories we tell ourselves.
These are the rules we live by.

LILITH. easy for you to say

OPPIE. Religion is...poetry.

LILITH. tribes and sides. a recipe for bloodshed.

OPPIE. Patterns. Stories of instruction. How we live with one another—

LILITH. no "we" without "they."

OPPIE. And then one day in Germany it's not shattered windows anymore it's not the ghetto anymore it's a sky full of thick black smoke
a cloud of human ash

And you wonder how this chain reaction ever started.

Wartime reparations + unemployment + directionless hatred given direction = critical mass.

And it all breaks apart. Atoms tear open. Your family is incinerated. *(He looks away. A long beat.)*

Your colleagues from Leipzig and Munich and Berlin
come here to live in pasteboard houses in the desert.

*(TELLER strides onstage, looking for someplace to put
his valise.)*

OPPIE. Edward! I'm so glad you could make it.
   Here we have gathered all the best scientific minds—
TELLER. Well, now that I am here. Yes.

THE GUN METHOD

*(OPPIE stands with a piece of chalk before the assem-
bled scientists.)*

OPPIE. This is what we know.
   Uranium 235 is our fissionable material.
   (He begins drawing on the board.)
   We believe the critical mass is 15 kilograms. Beyond
   that, the chain reaction begins—we have a great deal of
   energy released from the material.

   At the moment, we have approximately three table-
   spoons of Uranium 235. But that's not our worry. Two
   laboratories at other locations are working full time to
   separate out sufficient material. Our job is the design of
   the device.

   *(OPPIE sketches on the board. We see a cutaway of the
   bomb "Little Boy.")*

The plan thus far: inside the bomb's casing, we have a modified artillery gun, which fires the uranium shy, like a large bullet, into the subcritical uranium target. When the two subcritical uranium pieces come together, they exceed critical mass, and a nuclear explosion takes place.

Unless the speed is insufficient, in which case surface reactions blow the bomb apart before it goes fully critical.

(The YOUNG SCIENTIST stands up.)

YOUNG SCIENTIST. Oppie—what if. What if we shaped the fissionable material into a hollow sphere.

(Interested, OPPIE motions him forward, hands him the chalk. YOUNG SCIENTIST begins to draw excitedly as he talks.)

A hollow sphere…surrounded by explosive.

So that… Implosion. Implosion creates the critical mass.

RABI. You might need significantly less fissionable material.
   And the assemblage should be almost
RABI & YOUNG SCIENTIST. Instantaneous!
RABI. Certainly faster than the gun method.
OPPIE *(overlapping)*. Yes…yes… *(Beat.)* But the explosion is bound to be at least slightly asymmetrical. Might that cause a spurting of the fissionable material at the

point of weakness, again blowing the bomb apart before the chain reaction is established?

YOUNG SCIENTIST *(somewhat discouraged)*. Well... You're right, of course.

It would have to be absolutely symmetrical.

OPPIE. Good.

You work on that. *(The YOUNG SCIENTIST beams.)*
We will also continue work on the gun method. Both have possibilities to succeed.

(TELLER, who has been scribbling madly for a while, bursts out:)

TELLER. The tremendous heat released by *fission* should be sufficient to cause the even greater—
a FUSION reaction. Not just breaking apart—the atoms FUSE to make a NEW ELEMENT, meanwhile they release TREMENDOUS FORCE OF ENERGY.

OPPIE. Yes. I suppose if you could create an environment where you could produce the fusion of two atoms, that would—

TELLER. THAT would be a REALLY BIG BOMB. A SUPER-BOMB.

OPPIE. Yes, well—

TELLER. Beyond Nuclear. A THERMO-NUCLEAR RE-ACTION.

OPPIE. Yes, Edward, but we don't have the nuclear reaction yet. That's really what we're all here to—

TELLER *(shrugs)*. An engineering problem.
You will find it.
I will work on my Super.
Deuterium. Deuterium could work...

(They disappear. OPPIE remains.)

OPPIE. All these bright minds.
  Shining.
LILITH. Glittering. Furious.
OPPIE *(shakes his head)*. Catching fire.
  Together.
  And we have everything we need.
  the laboratory
  has everything we need.
  Money does not curtail the experiment.
  None of us. Have ever known this
  freedom.
LILITH. freedom?
OPPIE *(looks at her)*. Yes.

(YOUNG SCIENTIST recites his letter. Elsewhere, a CENSOR, poised with a black marker.)

YOUNG SCIENTIST. Dear Mother:
  Outside, you can tell a world-class scientist by the Nobel
  Prize. In here, he rates a Bathtub. The rest of us are,
  quite literally, the great unwashed. *(CENSOR looks sus-
  picious, decides to leave it.)*
  Dr. (mm-mrf) brought his piano. *(CENSOR wields the
  marker.)*
  The weather is gorgeous. I never knew the sky could be
  so big.
  Would love to tell you more, but you know they
  (mmrf-rf) our mail.
  your loving son,

GROVES

GROVES. You said thirty.
  Thirty scientists and their families.

  What we have here is a city. Six thousand people. On your project.

  I've spent half a billion dollars. On your project.

  What I want to know is.

  Are you any closer? To making it work?
OPPIE. Yes—always closer.
GROVES. Tell me again.
OPPIE. It's going to work.
GROVES. I'm putting that in my report.

  (GROVES exits, passing an area with LANSDALE and the CENSOR.)

CENSOR. Sir? They won't stop mentioning the censorship in their letters home…
GROVES. Well, keep cutting it out.
CENSOR. Yes, sir.
LANSDALE *(with a sense of humor)*. It's top secret that this place is so secret we need to censor the mail. The censorship itself is somehow not considered a dead give-away. *(GROVES looks at him sharply.)*
  Sir.

JULIUS

LILITH. Julius.
  Julius.
OPPIE. It's just J.
LILITH. It stands for Julius. Your father's name.
OPPIE. It stands for nothing.
LILITH. The tailor's name.
OPPIE. He imported cloth.
LILITH. You called him that. Called yourself the tailor's son. Very sensitive about that.
OPPIE. Yes.
LILITH. You were a spoiled little brat.
OPPIE *(smiling)*. There are those who say I still am.
LILITH. It bothered you that the money came from somewhere?
OPPIE. I suppose
LILITH. That it wasn't just shit by God.
  That in fact, you came from a long line of cross-legged, squinting Jews. Pushing needle through cloth. Davening closer to the light to see the tiny stitches. Putting their gold in little purses hidden up in the mattress ticking. In case the Pogrom, in case the Cossacks came again. Building up coin upon coin so that Julius could get out.
  Come to America.
  Do very well.

  So that Julius' son could walk down the street, head held high. Never know the squint and stoop that put him there.

GIBSONS

(Spot on KITTY.)

KITTY. I did as you asked, darling. I had some of the Women over.
I was an excellent hostess.
Cooked up something elaborate.
Gibsons.

They'd just gotten those little cocktail onions in at the PX, and I thought I'd take advantage.

We drank quietly for an hour or so and then everyone went home.
It was truly dreadful.

I'll do it again, if you like.

But I think you should get someone else to play Director's Wife.

TELLER REPLACED BY FUCHS

OPPIE. Edward, I'm glad you're here— I've had several... requests. I must ask you to stop playing the piano at all hours.

TELLER. It helps me think.

RABI. You know what helps me think? Sleeping! For at least a few blasted hours a night.

TELLER. I'M WORKING.

RABI. Not on our project!

TELLER. I cannot— Look. Here. My Super is of primary importance.

RABI. This is what I've been telling you, Oppie. He's absolutely— *(Stops himself, finishes:)*
unhelpful.

OPPIE. Well, the British are sending some men over. I'll
get you a replacement. *(Scans some papers.)*
Uh...Klaus Fuchs will join your team. Edward, you're
all right on your own?

TELLER. Preferably.

OPPIE. Good. Then it's settled.

*(The YOUNG SCIENTIST enters, holding a mangled
pipe.)*

YOUNG SCIENTIST. Oppie?
I thought I'd start with a cylinder, since that's easier
than a sphere, but implosion is far from even, no matter
what I—

OPPIE *(cold)*. Have I picked the wrong man for this job?

YOUNG SCIENTIST. I just... Maybe. I just don't know if
it can be done.

OPPIE. It was YOUR idea.
YOU make it work. *(Blackout. OPPIE.)*

LILITH. Julius.
J.
J. Robert.
Are you angry at him?
Or yoursssssself?

OPPIE *(smiles)*. You're worse than my clearance board.

LILITH. They could never get inside your head. Understand what made you tick tick tick tick tick tick tick tick
tick. Their inquiry stopped at the ice-blue eyes. While I.
Have been inside your head a long, long time.

JEAN

(OPPIE sits, sketching on a pad of paper. Possibly, we see diagrams sketched out behind him.)

OPPIE *(muttering)*. A hollow sphere of subcritical material. Less than 5% variation in symmetry of the shockwave. Otherwise— *(Phone rings. He jumps, picks it up.)*
JEAN'S VOICE. Robert. I have to see you.
OPPIE. Jean. I can't.

(An image: JEAN. She chases down a few pills with a glass of water.)

JEAN. I must. see you.
(In another area: two SECURITY AGENTS become visible, listening in, taking notes.)
Robert.
OPPIE. I'll see what I can do.

(He hangs up the phone. JEAN takes a shuddering breath, hangs up. She turns on the radio, it plays a slow, mournful waltz, which she dances vaguely to.)

SECURITY ONE. subject: Jean Tatlock.
SECURITY TWO. That Red tart again.
SECURITY ONE. Dr. Oppenheimer received call at 21:00 hours.
SECURITY TWO. You think she's pumping him for info?
SECURITY ONE. While he's pumping her?
SECURITY TWO. I heard those communist babes are hot.
SECURITY ONE. Yeah?

SECURITY TWO. *Red* hot.
SECURITY ONE. shaddup an transcribe the tape.
LILITH. And did you see her?
OPPIE. Once.
LILITH. And did you inform Security?
OPPIE. It was not. A government matter.

   They informed me, later. Of her suicide.
   (JEAN stares at him, smoking a cigarette.)
   You look beautiful.
JEAN *(smiles grandly)*. Thank you. I feel like shit. *(Beat.)*
   Didn't think I was ever going to see you again.
   What's so god-damned important that you can't—
OPPIE. I can't tell you.
JEAN. Right.
OPPIE. I have to go back.
JEAN. Your Country needs you?
OPPIE. Yes.
JEAN. And your wife?
OPPIE. You didn't want to marry me—
JEAN. I wasn't pregnant.
OPPIE. you won't let me go.
JEAN. Can't. There is a difference.
OPPIE. As if you'd know. You've never done a thing that
   wasn't precisely your current whim—
JEAN. That's right. I'm nothing but a spoiled little dilet-
   tante with a bleeding heart and a bottle of prescription
   pills. *(Beat. Soft.)*
OPPIE. I have to go back.
JEAN. You can go in the morning.
   Can't you?
OPPIE. All right.

(He goes to her. Strokes her hair. She leans her face against his chest. Lights fade on them.

LILITH eats something.

Wipes blood from her mouth in a smear across her cheek. Pulls a tiny bone from her mouth.

Laboratory.

The three SCIENTISTS, muttering and pacing in circles, à la the Marx Brothers.)

TELLER. Deuterium.

RABI. Deuterium.

YOUNG SCIENTIST. Deuterium.

TELLER. Lithium…

RABI. Lithium.

YOUNG SCIENTIST. For him, or the bomb?

RABI. Shhhh.

TELLER *(eureka)*. Lithium Deuteride! *(They all rush to the board and begin calculating.)*
Lithium Deuteride…with an atomic bomb ignition of the Tritium…

YOUNG SCIENTIST. According to the new calculations, how heavy will this bomb be?

TELLER *(does some quick addition in his head)*. Five hundred tons. *(Beat. They all consider this.)*
A plutonium-powered superplane to drop it, perhaps.
Get some engineers on that.

RABI. Perhaps we should return to the problem of fission—

TELLER *(banishes him)*. OUT!

(OPPIE. The desert.)

OPPIE. The first time I saw these mountains I was a boy.
LILITH. A city boy.
OPPIE. The world was contained in the pages of a book for me, and here it was opening up before me like…the world.

I'd asked him if we could say I was his younger brother. For the trip.
He said no.

I had worked too hard, at too high a pitch, and my body collapsed. The whole point had been to attend Harvard at sixteen, but…

This year. My parents paid my favorite teacher to take an extended trip with me. To the Sangre de Christo mountains. To get back my strength.

It was a wonderful time. On horseback I was…fearless.

All went well. Very well. Then one day we had to get an early start, and he had not finished packing. He asked me to fold his coat for him.

Tossed it across the room to me. Bent to continue packing.

My knuckles went white in the cloth.

I said, that's right, give it to the Tailor's son. He'll fold it.

The look of shock. Hurt, even. That I would think such a thing.

I regretted the words the instant they were out of my mouth.

But that doesn't mean they weren't true.

LILITH. As he shook his blonde head, sadly

OPPIE. I never said he was blonde.

LILITH. Was he better than your father, to model yourself on?

OPPIE. Horseback riding down a ravine. Shoulders thrown back.

Never a shrug, never an apology. Who would you choose?

(Another area: LANSDALE, handing GENERAL GROVES a file.)

LANSDALE. Here it is, sir.

(JEAN appears in back. She places cushions in front of a bathtub, then begins, slowly and methodically, to take a large handful of pills. OPPIE watches this.)

In the last position we captured, we found the laboratory. What was left of it. They were still all working away, in the midst of, well, a lot of rubble, sir. Amazing, when you compare it with what we've got here.

They were questioned over the course of twenty-four hours, all together and separately.

The information is conclusive.

Germany is no longer working toward an atomic weapon. *(GROVES is still reading.)*

So.

Shall we tell our guys?

GROVES. No.

LANSDALE. No?

GROVES. No. Gotta keep the fire under the jew-boys.

(JEAN walks carefully to the bathtub.)

If they don't come up with it, I've sunk over a billion dollars of the Army's money into the biggest dud in history. It's *my* ass on the line.

LANSDALE. Yes, sir.

GROVES. These scientists think small.

Hitler and their calculations working out. That's about it.

(JEAN kneels on the cushions)

They're not going to understand about America's needing to be the most powerfully armed nation in the world.

They're not looking ahead to the next conflict.

Which is likely to be with our Allies, the Soviets.

After the smoke clears.

And they shut down the ovens.

No, we need the little man with the moustache.

He's going to get us our bomb.

Keep a fire under them until it's too late.

LANSDALE. Too late?

(JEAN plunges her head into the water.)

GROVES. Soon, there'll be no stopping.

They'll have to *know* if the experiment works.

LANSDALE *(startled)*. Experiment?

GROVES. If they get close enough, they'll forget it was ever anything else.

(GROVES smiles. A cool, frightening smile.

Blackout on them.

JEAN. Head underwater. For a long time.)

LILITH. How long is she in the bath?
OPPIE. Four days.
Her…her father found her. *(With great effort, looks away from JEAN.)*
A lovely man. A professor of English at Berkeley. When I went to his home, it seemed there were no walls. Nothing but books, everywhere. And the most beautiful girl. He introduced me to her. and she introduced me to… many things.
LILITH. Communism.
OPPIE. Yes. And frozen custard on the boardwalk at Coney Island.
LILITH. And the Metaphysics of John Donne.

(A gathering of SCIENTISTS. OPPIE is distracted.)

YOUNG SCIENTIST. I think we should let the Russians know what we've discovered—
RABI. An international sharing of knowledge. Like before the war.
OPPIE. I'm all for the sharing of our knowledge. But it must be done through the proper channels. It's for the President to decide, now. It's not peacetime anymore.
YOUNG SCIENTIST. But it will be again soon. We can go back to our lives, the way things were. Why shouldn't we let the Russians know what we've been doing?

TELLER *(incredulous). Why?* Why shouldn't we just give over what we have?

YOUNG SCIENTIST. But the Russians are our allies.

TELLER. Bah. Allies.

Only when it suits them.

YOUNG SCIENTIST. How can you say that? The Russians suffered more casualties—

TELLER. You did not see the Communists in Budapest.

And this peacetime? That you remember. Is never coming back.

OPPIE. Edward. I don't think there's any reason to paint so grim a picture.

TELLER. hmf.

OPPIE. Roosevelt will make the right decision.

LILITH. The wise and thoughtful Father of a Nation, curling you up for those Fireside Chats.

(Home. KITTY looks genuinely shaken.)

KITTY. What...will we do?

OPPIE. We?

KITTY. The country.

OPPIE. I don't know.

THE PRESIDENT IS DEAD

(OPPIE gives on-site eulogy for President Roosevelt.)

OPPIE. When, three days ago, the world had word of the death of President Roosevelt, many wept who are unaccustomed to tears, many men and women, little enough accustomed to prayer, prayed to God. Many of us looked with deep trouble to the future.

We have been living through years of great evil, and of great terror. Roosevelt has been our President, our Commander-in-Chief, our leader. All over the world men have seen symbolized in him their hope that the evils of this time would not be repeated; that the terrible sacrifices which have been made, and those that are still to be made, would lead to a world more fit for human habitation.

In the Hindu scripture, in the Bhagavad-Gita, it says, "Man is a creature whose substance is faith. What his faith is, he is." The faith of Roosevelt is one that is shared by millions of men and women, in every country of the world. For this reason it is possible to maintain the hope, that his good works will not have ended with his death. *(Turning suddenly to GROVES.)*
So Truman knew nothing of the Project?

GROVES. Only the President.
(Exiting.) Don't worry, I'll explain it all to him.

OPPIE. That's not what I'm worried about.

KITTY *(accosts him)*. I'm glad she's dead. *(OPPIE doesn't answer.)* You hear me?

OPPIE. What makes you think I didn't hear.

KITTY. I don't know, I thought maybe you'd hit me or something. Defend her honor.

OPPIE. I'm going out.

KITTY. At least now I know you'll come back.

OPPIE. I would never have left you. I take the marriage vows seriously.

KITTY. AND I DON'T?

OPPIE. Upon third recitation, the words become true? How like a fairytale.

KITTY. Get out.

(When he's at the door.) You leave me I'll fuck those kids up like you wouldn't believe.

OPPIE. *If* I leave?

(OPPIE stalks out. KITTY takes a deep breath. Releases it slowly. Runs a hand through her hair. Outside. OPPIE runs into the YOUNG SCIENTIST, holding another badly mangled pipe.)

YOUNG SCIENTIST. Oppie, I—

OPPIE. FIX IT.

LILITH. those days before Trinity
    you lived on smoke
    down to 115 pounds. Six feet tall, weighing no more than a girl

    I could lift you in a breath

    lived on smoke

    and the bright-burning fires in your head.

OPPIE. yes.

LILITH. fury.

OPPIE. discovery.

LILITH. only hate burns that bright
    don't lie to me
    I could smell it

OPPIE. I don't lie
    to you

LILITH. I know by now the smell of burning hate

it comes from my heart
up into my nostrils
every day
the sun rises and hits me, smoldering

(Laboratory.

OPPIE watches an experiment.

Late night, SCIENTISTS with their shirtsleeves rolled up. There is an aura of holiness to these rituals, this work. Occasionally one glances at OPPIE. They are glad he's there. Watching them, watching over them. Under everything, the low-level clicks of a geiger counter.

Small pieces of metal are placed, one by one, into a pile. The geiger counter leaps into an alarming fuzz of rapid, almost indistinguishable clicks. The last piece is quickly removed—the geiger counter calms. It is replaced by a much smaller piece. And another. And another. The geiger counter starts up again. The last piece is removed. It is replaced by a smaller one. The geiger counter starts up. It is removed. There is some laughter, relief. Numbers are recorded. OPPIE smiles, gets his coat. Administers pats on the back on his way out.)

(Home. OPPIE comes in, quietly. It's very late. KITTY is waiting up.)

KITTY. Non-aggression pact?
OPPIE *(smiles)*. All right.
    Kids asleep?
KITTY. It's three-thirty in the morning.

OPPIE. Oh.

We were…"tickling the dragon's taii."

KITTY. Is it as dangerous as all that?

OPPIE *(a light laugh, with an edge of wonder. then:)*. yes.

KITTY. You're careful?

OPPIE. We're careful. *(He goes to her. They kiss.)*

Why this…détente?

KITTY. You didn't hear?

OPPIE. We didn't have the radio on…

KITTY. Darling, it's…

Victory in Europe.

OPPIE *(a beat)*. Good.

KITTY. Good?

OPPIE. It's not over yet. The focus will shift to the Pacific.

KITTY. Yes. But.

It's a day of great jubilation. They said so on the radio.

(They embrace. OPPIE kisses the top of her head.)

OPPIE. All right. It's a day of great jubilation.

LILITH. LIAR!

KITTY. I'm exhausted. Come to bed?

OPPIE. Yes. *(She exits.)*

LILITH. Well there you go. Hitler is vanquished. Kiss your
wife and take her home.

hmmm?

oppie oppie oppie.

so Disappointed—

OPPIE. No—

LILITH. Don't lie to me!

OPPIE. It's…very complicated.

LILITH *(clicks at him)*. complicated?

OPPIE. We—we wanted to have done something!
   All right?

LILITH *(smiles)*. Yesssssss

OPPIE. perhaps we should have stopped then.

LILITH. but you didn't

OPPIE. no.

LILITH. you worked harder.

OPPIE. Unabated. We did not slack off in our pursuit of the atomic bomb.

LILITH. you worked harder.

OPPIE. perhaps.

LILITH. You didn't want the war to end before you'd got your gadget complete.

OPPIE. we were getting very close to success.

LILITH. succccccesssss

OPPIE. *tantalizingly* close

LILITH. yessssss
   someone had to pay.

OPPIE. *No*. that's not—

LILITH. Come *on*…

OPPIE. Practice!
   The theory was impeccable, but we could have over-looked something. maybe—

   We *had* to see…if it would work.

SCIENTIST ONE. Implosion's not working.

SCIENTIST TWO. The blast is uneven.

SCIENTIST THREE. The detonating lenses are pitted! The molds didn't work—

SCIENTIST ONE. I did the calculations. It's not going to work.

OPPIE. It's got to. That's all.

REPORTER

(An army Press Corps REPORTER hovers at OPPEN-HEIMER's elbow.)

REPORTER. I sent out the press releases.

OPPIE. Nothing's happened yet.

REPORTER. I sent three. They'll release whichever one's appropriate.

OPPIE *(distracted)*. Ah. Good planning.

REPORTER. One, an ammunition shed accidentally went off. No one was injured.

Two, a large munitions dump accidentally went off. Some people were injured.

Three, there was a freak accident at Dr. Oppenheimer's ranch, where he was hosting a gathering of eminent scientific friends for his birthday.

That one has all of our obituaries.

VOICEOVER. Dr. Oppenheimer. It's time for the test.

(TELLER puts on suntan lotion. RABI and YOUNG SCIENTIST don dark goggles.)

THE BLAST

VOICEOVER. Ten.

Nine.

Eight.

Seven. *(Etc.)*

OPPIE. A local station broke in on our frequency.

They were playing

(Again, we hear the opening bars of the Nutcracker Suite.)

The Nutcracker Suite.

VOICEOVER. One.

(Slowly, a blast of pure white light. Then the sound, like thunder but continuous, rolling in from a long way away.)

OPPIE. The hundred-foot tower we'd constructed to hold it was vaporized.

The heat from the blast melted the sand.

Fused it into a beautiful green glass, which we named Trinitite.

*

It was, of course, highly radioactive.

*LILITH *(sings)*.

Green glass, greenglass. Green glass, greenglass. green glass.

OPPIE. We did it.

WE DID IT.

LILITH. And you didn't ignite the oxygen in the air

OPPIE. Nitrogen was the concern—

LILITH. well you didn't blow it up

OPPIE. and the thing worked!

after all that.

It worked.

All the calculations

the fifteen-hour days, the eighteen-hour days

LILITH. tasting blood on every cigarette from your own gums

OPPIE. the greatest scientific undertaking ever—

LILITH. it worked.

Ssssssso the next quesstion is.

OPPIE. What do we do with it? *(LILITH echoes.)*

WHAT DO WE DO WITH IT?

YOUNG SCIENTIST. There could be a test, very much like this one, in an unpopulated area of a neutral country, perhaps. And Japanese heads of state could be invited…

OPPIE *(to YOUNG SCIENTIST)*.

And what if it doesn't go off?

What if that one's a dud?

We've invited the Japanese heads of state to witness our embarrassment.

YOUNG SCIENTIST *(bright, joking)*.

Then we'll just kill 'em all!

OPPIE. I'll bring it up at the committee meeting.

LILITH. And the committee said:

OPPIE. We can propose no technical demonstration likely to bring an end to the war… We find no acceptable alternative to direct military use.

LILITH. mmmmmm.

and whose words are those?

OPPIE. mine.

LILITH. words out of your head

like the beautiful explosion

out of your head

that was the first time I took notice of you

oppie

such a beautiful man

head so full of poison
so full of a thing about to explode

OPPIE. The Interim Committee recommends:

    1. That the bomb should be used against Japan.

    2. That the target should be a military one surrounded by a civilian population.

    3. That the bomb be dropped without any prior warning.

(A flash of light. A tremendous explosion.)

LILITH. *HIROSHIMA.*

VOICEOVER. phone call from General Groves for Dr. Oppenheimer.

GROVES. *I'm very proud of you and all your people.*

OPPIE. *It went all right?*

GROVES. *Apparently it went with a tremendous bang.*

LILITH. I watched it explode and burn, curling black in the terrible, beautiful heat. The heat from inside your head. I watched the black death and death and death, breathed it in. I breathed Auschwitz, Dachau, Birkenau. Pogrom after century of pogrom. Huddled, whispering in secret in Egypt, marking our doors with the bloody lamb-bone. Begging for a scrap of God's mercy. I watched it burn and burn and burn

and I said *DO IT AGAIN! DO IT AGAIN! DO IT AGAIN.*

(Soft breaths.)

na

ga

sa

ki

(Getting tired.)
make another one.
bigger
(Cries, like a child and not like a child.)
do it again

HIROSHIMA PARTY

(Music of a party. OPPENHEIMER walks out to look at the stars, martini in hand. The YOUNG SCIENTIST is retching into the bushes.)

OPPIE. Little much to drink?
YOUNG SCIENTIST. no, sir. Nothing.

it's just…
OPPIE. What?
YOUNG SCIENTIST. That ammunitions ship that blew up in Halifax. 1917. Five thousand tons of TNT.
OPPIE. yes.
YOUNG SCIENTIST. Two and a half square miles destroyed. Four thousand people dead.
Trinity was—
OPPIE *(nodding)*. Fifteen thousand tons.
YOUNG SCIENTIST. And Hiroshima is far more densely populated than Halifax in 1917. So the number of casualties—
OPPIE. Don't do the calculations.
YOUNG SCIENTIST. The…the Physics.

It's not *theoretical* anymore, is it?
OPPIE *(soft)*. no, it's not.

TELLER *(enters, drink in hand).* So—a good show today.
   And now it is begun.
LILITH. and when does the next one go down?
OPPIE. The Japanese are so stubborn—
LILITH. Once again, President Truman tells the Japanese
   to surrender unconditionally or "expect a rain of ruin
   from the air, the like of which has never been seen on
   this earth."

   Reports came through from Hiroshima but they were not
   believed. So the emperor sssent envoys to ssseeee. The
   truth. To sseee that a ssingle bomb had leveled his city.
   the gathering and relay of this information took 52 hours.
   by which time the bomber captain had decided it was
   time to drop the other
   because the weather was just perfect
   to dessstroy a city.

   80,000 dead in Nagasaki.
   Fat Man. Duplicate of the plutonium implosion model
   tested at Trinity

   What's a Jew doing naming it Trinity?
OPPIE. I'd been reading Donne.
LILITH. Batter my heart, three person'd God
OPPIE. And another, written just before his death.

   "As West and East
   in all flat maps—and I am one—are one
   So death doth touch the Resurrection."
   (LILITH clicks at him.)
   And now—
   the fallout—

*(YOUNG SCIENTIST walks across the stage with a gei-
ger counter. It registers higher and lower, but never silence.)*

YOUNG SCIENTIST. We didn't really think about the
fallout.

RABI. Didn't really think about the fallout?

YOUNG SCIENTIST. We thought there might not be any
fallout.

RABI. How could there not be any fallout?

YOUNG SCIENTIST. We didn't know if it was going to
go off. *(Beat.)*

RABI. Right.

OPPIE. Cattle started showing up looking as if they'd had
a light dusting of snow.
Radiation burns. The hair grew back in white.

All around the test site...the ranches we had commandeered. the army had commandeered. Telling people
they'd get their land back after the war. Lingering radiation made the water undrinkable.

We'd poisoned the wells.

(TELLER bursts in)

TELLER. We must Immediately begin production for my
SUPER. The THERMONUCLEAR DEVICE.

OPPIE. They've surrendered. Let's just—

TELLER. It must be done.

OPPIE. get back to our lives. The Universities.

TELLER. IT CAN BE DONE.

Someone will do it.

Therefore, it must be done.

OPPIE. Edward, I don't even know if it *can* be done.

TELLER. IT MUST.

OPPIE. The war is over. *(Lights down to a spot on OPPIE.)*
  The war is over.

  Kitty…
  what have I done?

KITTY *(very gently)*. What needed to be done.
  Drink?

OPPIE. Thank you, darling. *(KITTY exits.)*

LILITH. *Is it perfume from a dress that makes me so digress?*

OPPIE. Mm?

LILITH. What's in your ticky little mind?

OPPIE. a different time.
  When I was less comfortable in a roomful of men and
  women.
  A time when I would just as soon leave a party as—

*(A sudden burst of cocktail party music and chatter.
KITTY reenters, wearing an elegant but sexy little cocktail dress, a drink in each hand. She gives him one.)*

OPPIE. I'm sorry?

KITTY. I said, it's a great shame I'm married.

OPPIE. Why?

KITTY. Because I find you very attractive, Dr. Oppenheimer. *(OPPIE blushes.)* I'm sorry. Did I shock you?

OPPIE. No…no…

KITTY. I'm like that. Just blunder my way through any so-
  cial situation. That's why I make it a point to dress well.

It helps people overlook what I've said when we've all sobered up.

OPPIE. I'm not planning on sobering up.

KITTY. Good for you!

OPPIE. No, I mean…I'm not drunk.

KITTY. Well, what are you waiting for? The night is young and you're with another man's wife.

OPPIE. I would have to agree with you.

KITTY. Shall we make our way to the drinks, then?

OPPIE. I would have to agree with you that it is a great shame. That you are married.

KITTY. Well, perhaps there's still hope of shocking you, Dr. Oppenheimer.

(She lowers her voice to a stage whisper.)

It's not an incurable state. Marriage.

(She looks to see if he's shocked.)

OPPIE. Robert. Please call me Robert.

KITTY. Kitty.

(She presents her hand.) Charmed, I'm sure.

OPPIE. I'm not sure of much, right now.

KITTY. Well then.

You must be Charmed. *(Party fades.)*

LILITH. A charmed life.

To cause the deaths of so many.

OPPIE. The greatest scientific undertaking…ever.

And in the end, it was for this.

A blast with the light of a thousand suns.

Finally brought that… Unconditional Surrender.

(JEAN appears. Drowned. OPPIE starts, takes a step toward her. She opens her mouth to speak. Water pours

*out. OPPIE rubs his eyes, one hand squeezed over them,
massaging his temples. She recedes into the shadows.)*

I had wanted...
We had all wanted.
To know.
What would happen.
LILITH. sssseeeeking knowledge?
OPPIE. yes
LILITH. and?
OPPIE. And to stop Hitler, of course. It was of the utmost
importance that we find this knowledge before he did.

Knowledge had always been implicitly good. Now this
very premise must be questioned.

I have...blood on my hands.

What if you
what if you spend your life in pursuit of knowledge and it

unleashes a great destructive force upon the world

and not even on Hitler but on—

what if you spend all your time and thoughts and breath
and life creating this great destructive force and you
wish you had never unleashed the fury inside those at-
oms? Let Uranium 235 remain sovereign and unbroken.
Not opened that box?
LILITH. I've heard all this ssssssomewhere before.
God says
I've got this great idea
I'm going to make a woman
out of dirt

and breathe into her nostrils and look how beautiful
SHE LIVES.
Adam and Lilith, my playthings. I breathed my wet
God-breath into their little dirt mouths and look at the
mud things walking around naming the beasts, eating the
plants.

then Adam says to me LIE DOWN
as if we were not both the same
he says LIE DOWN I WANT TO
and I say, hey, wait a minute here, I'm not saying let's
not have fun, but what makes you the one to climb up
on top of me? I don't think this is really about sex here I
don't think this is about exploring these new bodies with
the new wet life breathed in I think this is about you trying to get on top of me
LIE DOWN
I think you want to hold me there
LIE DOWN
He would not stop saying it and his face all red
LIE DOWN
Grabbed both my arms and tried to knock me down in
the dirt we'd both come from.

I spoke the sacred name of God and flew up into the sky.

Went off on my own, to the shores of the Red Sea. Till
he thought better of his behavior.
We're all learning here, after all.

But Adam
Adam goes to God and he complains
that I will not lie down and God says

What?

Don't worry, little man
I will make you a new one.

I will rip open your side

and take from you
since you would not take what I made you the first time

(and I thought, made You?)
let me rip a piece from you
close to the heart

now I take this dripping bloody piece of you and I make
you a woman who will lie down. She will do nothing
but lie down.
she will lie down for you.

and to me he says
eat their babies.
They are delicious.

Especially the red-brown marrow in the troughs of their
white bones.

TELLER. WE MUST MAKE MY SUPER.
    Nothing changes. Don't go—
OPPIE. We're going home.
    everyone is going home.

*(Light on YOUNG SCIENTIST, placing plutonium cubes
carefully atop a pile)*

YOUNG SCIENTIST. Before we go

just a few final *(Removes a large cube from the bottom, adds a small one on top.)*
calculations *(Drops the large cube onto the pile. The room is instantly suffused with a blue glow. The geiger counters go crazy.)*
ah! *(He knocks this final cube off the pile. The blue glow stops, the clicking is silenced.)*

That was a close one!
Did…
did anyone get a reading on that?

(Blackout. Sound of decontamination showers.

Makeshift hospital: Los Alamos. The YOUNG SCIENTIST lies, oxygen-tented, in a hospital bed. Sound of labored breathing. OPPENHEIMER sits at his bedside, reading from a small book.)

OPPIE. *Our bodies are known to end,*
but the embodied self is enduring,
indestructible, and immeasurable;
therefore, Arjuna, fight the battle!

As a man discards
worn-out clothes
to put on new ones,
so the embodied self
discards
its worn-out bodies
to take on other new ones.

Weapons do not cut it,
fire does not burn it,

waters do not wet it,
wind does not wither it.
If you think of its birth
and death as ever-recurring,
then too, Great Warrior,
you have no cause to grieve.

(OPPIE wipes at his eyes.)

NURSE. Perhaps you should go now, Dr. Oppenheimer. He should rest.

OPPIE. You think I'm keeping him awake?

NURSE *(gently)*. I think you should get some sleep, actually.

OPPIE. Oh.

I suppose…

That's…very kind of you. *(OPPIE and the NURSE move away from the bedside.)*

NURSE. I thought that Jews had the same Bible, or the first part, anyway.

OPPIE *(absently)*. Yes, they do.

NURSE. What was that, then?

OPPIE. One of the sacred Hindu texts.

It's Krishna's instructions to the warrior Arjuna, who… hesitates on the battlefield.

NURSE. And you believe that stuff?

OPPIE. I find it…beautiful.

There are those who would say that makes it true. I… cannot. *(He puts on his coat.)*

I can prove it with Matter.

NURSE. What?

OPPIE. Neither created nor destroyed.

(NURSE nods. She's heard this before.)
You… You've seen this before.
You've seen men die.
You've seen babies take that first breath into their lungs
(He is desperate, searching.)
You tell me. Is it the same?
Are we never…destroyed…utterly?
NURSE *(looks at him)*. You're right, Dr. Oppenheimer.
OPPIE. What?
NURSE. It's a nice idea. *(Noise. Breathing more labored.)*
   You'd better go.

(NURSE disappears. OPPIE stares. Light out on the hospital scene. OPPIE's shoulders collapse. He seems to sink into himself. Covers his face with his hands. LILITH arrives to collect him.)

LILITH. Oppie.
   One death?
   You are a sentimentalist.
OPPIE. It's my fault.
LILITH. Many things are your fault.
OPPIE. And the pictures started coming back.
   Horrible, horrible things.

(Mother appears, wearing a kimono. Her back is to us.)

Kimono burns. The embroidery thread burned the flowers directly onto their skins.

(TELLER appears, crouched over a small seismograph. He stares at it intently.)

Among the photos brought back from Hiroshima, there was a woman. Severe burns. She was missing three fingers from her right hand. *(Slowly, elegantly, Mother begins to pull off her gloves.)* I know it doesn't mean anything. Still. It struck me. *(As she removes the second one: Blackout.)*

INTERMISSION

ACT II

(TELLER appears, with a kimono as a dressing-gown, over his clothes. He has a basin, a shaving-brush, a cake of soap.)

TELLER. Ah. If a thing is to be done.
It should be done properly. *(He creates lather, taking time and pleasure with this routine; lathers up and begins to shave with a straight-razor.)*
You see, Oppie, you are not the only one with a refined sensibility. You do not have a patent on the understanding of beauty.
And certainly not of truth.

I am the one who knows. Who always knew.
I drove Szilard to Einstein, in my old Plymouth, beat up and sputtering, stopping to ask directions of a child along the way. I got him to Einstein, to sign the letter to FDR warning
what the Germans were about to do
While you taught worshipful graduate students the correct wine to choose with dinner.

Who is better equipped to see what is needed?
I know what this country my adopted country, needs.

I will protect this country from Communism. From Fascism. From any threat. Because I am willing to do the ugly thing. First.

I have been accused of being a monomaniac. I ask you. Could a monomaniac play the piano like this? *(He plays Mozart's Eine Kleine Nachtmusik, the fist two phrases delicately, but he cannot resist playing the third with great force and bombast.)*
Ha.
They do not know me.
Or else they underestimate me. All of them. All the thems. Out there, who do not know.

Opje, they say you do not suffer fools gladly. But you do. You suffer them. More gladly than I. I can't suffer them at all. Not at all. No more fools for me. Suffering, I will take gladly. But not fools.
There are so many fools these days.
And Opje, you are the worst.
Because they listen to you.
You make fools of all the rest.
This I will not suffer. My community to be made fools, every one. Fools for Russia. SHE IS DANGEROUS. YOU FOOLS.

A young boy. Is working on a layer cake. Mother Russia, with her Russian Dolls, one inside another inside another inside another. She's got one in the oven. Ja. Uranium wrapped in Lithium Deuteride. Wrapped in Uranium. So on. Frosted in high-impact explosive.
A young boy named Sakharov has no one telling him to stop. No one telling him, We must not do this thing.

He is building his layer cake. To bring this country to its knees.

Later he will be sorry and sad. He will be a dissident. A fool like you, Opje.
But only after he's made it work.

When all fools get their conscience caught up. After the moment of discovery.
After coition, man sighs. And thinks and is sad.
After it's too late.
The woman understands the moment to hesitate is before, not after.
After is too late.

Does this help me? None at all. Helps me none at all.

I will be alone. All "good" men will turn their backs on me.
Because they say I stabbed you there, Opje.
You should not have turned away.

You knew the knife was in my hand. You should have helped me to wield it. And protect this great country. This country that you profess to love.
You should not have turned from me.
From this idea that must now be born. It is in my head. It is in Sakharov's. In layer upon layer in his mind. It was in Klaus Fuchs'. The head that he took with him each time he met his Russian contact, in Santa Fe, New Mexico. In a coffee shop in New York. In a pub in London. That big head went along. Full of secrets.
Klaus, he is very good at keeping secrets.
Ja.

And passing them like notes in school. He has a crush on the Soviet Union. As so many of you do. Because you do not know her, Mother Russia. You do not know she breaks bones. You do not know the gulag is built with them.

This bomb must happen. I have seen it in my mind. It will happen.

And I will be cast out, before that first test. I will watch from the basement of my Berkeley lab, four in the morning, watching the tiny dot of light. The photo-seismograph. At precisely the test time, there is a tiny shudder. I almost think I have not seen it. But I have seen it. A tiny shudder.
The world's first thermo-nuclear reaction.
It is begun.

But that is later. *(He towels the last of the lather off his face.)*
Not now.
But soon.

(He exits, revealing OPPIE besieged by REPORTERS.)

REPORTERS *(overlapping).* Dr. Oppenheimer!
Dr. Oppenheimer!

(OPPIE squints in the newsreel camera light. Nods to one REPORTER.)

REPORTER. Dr. Oppenheimer, can you tell us what your first thoughts were upon seeing the explosion at Trinity?

OPPIE. We knew the world would not be the same.

A few people laughed. A few people cried. Most people were silent.

I remembered the line from the Hindu scriptures, the Bhagavad-Gita.

Vishnu is trying to persuade the prince that he should do his duty, and to impress him, takes on his multi-armed form and says Now I am become Death, the Destroyer of Worlds.

I suppose we all thought that, some way or another.

LILITH. Dessssssssssstroyer.

OPPIE. I need to make this stop.

Got to make it stop.

I have a responsibility to my country—

LILITH. *Your* country.

Do you really think it's yours?

OPPIE. Of course it is.

LILITH. The Jews have never had a country. Only the clothes on their back.

oppie oppie oppie.
so naïve
how does such a smart man
learn so little
from Hissssstory?

OPPIE ADDRESSES THE SCIENTISTS

OPPIE. The experience of war has left us with a legacy of concern. Nowhere is this troubled sense of responsibility more acute than among those who participated in the development of atomic energy for military purposes.

In some crude sense which no vulgarity, no humor, no over-statement can quite extinguish, the physicists have known sin; and this is a knowledge which they cannot lose.

LILITH. pissssssed a lot of people off that time

OPPIE. My first year at Cambridge, I…was under a great deal of strain. Over summer's break I went on holiday with friends to Corsica. We were to continue on to Sardinia, but I felt much refreshed and told my companions that I had to return to school immediately, as I'd left a poisoned apple on Professor Blackett's desk.

It was a metaphor. Rotten scholarship, not a nice gift for teacher. A bad paper.

I discovered later that my companions had missed the metaphor and worried that I'd cracked up for good.

LILITH. And now. Did you return?

Dare disturb the University?

OPPIE. How could I? *(Sits, beaten.)*

How could I?

PANDORA'S BOX

(RABI enters. Looks at him a moment.)

RABI. You should take Princeton.

(With a little shrug, a little smile.) It's a nice campus.

OPPIE *(looks at him)*. Things will never be the same.

RABI. No.

But perhaps…better? *(OPPIE looks away.)*

You remember, in the story. The last thing let out, after all the demons are set loose. The last thing to come out of Pandora's Box is hope.

The horror of this weapon is so shocking a thing—

OPPIE *(an awakening)*. You're right. People will see. People will have to understand.

LILITH. I always wondered.

With Pandora's Box.

Is Hope a good thing?

Or is that the final evil loosed upon the world.

That no matter what, you are cursed with this

Hope.

That things will turn out all right.

OPPIE. It's so clear—if all the countries of the world agree

never to produce these things again

instead of bombs

we make reactors

energy enough to light the darkness

irrigate the deserts

produce food

energy—the universal currency of production—will barely be an expense.

abundance, plenty, ease

these things are within our grasp

as a people

as a world *(LILITH laughs.)*

What?

LILITH *(kind)*. You're funny.

OPPIE. It's possible! Right now—

if we don't
lose this chance—
LILITH. not yours to lose
OPPIE *(urgent)*. yes
LILITH. It doesn't work.
OPPIE. what do you—
LILITH. It doesn't work.
There is no future of light and harmony and grace.
OPPIE. Maybe you're wrong.
LILITH *(shrugs)*. Maybe I am.
OPPIE. Can you see
everything?
LILITH. only flashes.
flashes of light. explosions.
they don't stop.
pain. the smell of blood. Women ripped open by the life
inside them. Thousands of times a day.
smell of gunpowder
smell of iron
smell of ozone
a lightning storm and the ground is soaked with blood
more of you grow out of this blood-soaked dirt
there is quiet for a while
and then it starts again
the explosions
blood and crying little wriggling things
with soft sweet bones
the explosions get bigger and bigger
the earth shakes and trembles
she is pitted in her deserts
in her oceans
choking smell of ozone the atmosphere is torn

like a woman's cunt
no time to heal in between
the explosions get bigger and bigger
and then tiny
but they never stop
so small
barely a pinprick
a girl straps explosives to her waist
and walks to the market
a bus splits in two
a marine barracks
an embassy
rhythm like a tapping
like a ticking
of something big
waiting to
explode.

OPPIE. STOP IT.

LILITH. Why do you fight?

OPPIE. IT STOPS. Here.

I will dedicate my life to it.

LILITH (*smiles*). one life…

REPORTERS (*overlapping*). Dr. Oppenheimer!

Dr. Oppenheimer!

OPPIE (*flooded with newsreel camera light*).

I have been asked whether in the years to come it will be possible to kill 40 million American people in the 20 largest American towns by the use of atomic bombs in a single night. I'm afraid the answer to that question is Yes.

Our only hope lies in international control of this force so great it could mean the death of all civilization.

(To LILITH.) People will see.

These are not weapons for war. These are weapons to stop war. Make it so hideous a thing it can no longer be contemplated.

LILITH. There is nothing so hideous it cannot be held within the confines of a human skull.

OPPIE. An appeal to people's better nature, the spirit of co-operation, and
WHAT'S SO FUNNY?

LILITH. When do you stop being a boy?

OPPIE. I was never a child as a child. I was always…this.

(JEAN becomes visible, lying down, reading the paper. The calm of a happier time. OPPIE starts, composes himself.)

LILITH. She's dead, you know.

OPPIE. I know.

LILITH. Pretty girl.

OPPIE *(snaps around to LILITH)*. leave me alone, can't you leave me alone for one damned minute? *(He turns around.)*

LILITH. Don't turn your back on me. You will regret it. *(She is gone.)*

OPPIE *(smiles)*. What's one more?

JEAN *(calls, not looking up from her paper)*. What did you say?

(OPPIE approaches her, strokes the gentle curve of her side.)

OPPIE. Did you know, in Sanskrit poetry, the poets always make reference to the great beauty of the three rolls of fat at the beloved's waist?

JEAN. What's that mean?

OPPIE. You wouldn't have been considered beautiful at all.

JEAN. Well, it's a good thing I'm not written in Sanskrit.

OPPIE. And lips like ripe bimba fruit.

JEAN. What *could* that mean?

OPPIE *(smiles)*. Red!

JEAN. Mmmm.

OPPIE *(shrugs)*. Lips like cherries, lips like bimba fruit…

JEAN. So the most beautiful women were great fat cows?

OPPIE. Beauty changes. Elizabethan women plucked their hairlines, as a high forehead was considered the zenith of beauty.

Of course, In modern times. You. Are the most beautiful woman in the world. *(JEAN makes an amused noise, continues reading.)* What are you reading?

JEAN. The People's World.

OPPIE. What people?

JEAN. The workers.

OPPIE. Oh, those people.

JEAN. Those who pick the bimba fruit. Or strawberries. Did you know the migrant workers call strawberries the Devil's Fruit. It's backbreaking labor, picking them off the ground all day. Bending from sunup to sundown.

OPPIE. Yes, it's terrible, the inequities of the world.

JEAN *(sits up, agitated)*. You say that. It's perfectly easy to say that. But are you willing to *do* something about it? There are people who—

Listen. I want you to come to a meeting with me—

(Lights up, harsh, on a Senate Committee Meeting.)

STRAUSS. But what of the Communist Menace?

INSULTS STRAUSS

(OPPENHEIMER testifies before a senate committee on the export of isotopes.)

STRAUSS. These ISOTOPES, that you claim would be perfectly safe to release to scientists in Norway, many of whom have KNOWN COMMUNIST CONTACTS. Isn't it true these ISOTOPES could be used by a Foreign Power to make their own atomic bomb?

OPPIE *(much put-upon by the ignorance around him).*
No one can force me to say you cannot use these isotopes for atomic energy. You can use a shovel for atomic energy. In fact you do. You can use a bottle of beer for atomic energy. In fact, you do. But the fact is that during the war and after the war these materials have played no significant part and in my knowledge no part at all. *(A ripple of laughter in the senate. STRAUSS turns purple with fury.)*
My own rating of the importance of isotopes in this broad sense is that they are far less important than electronic devices, but far more important than, let us say, vitamins, somewhere in between. *(More laughter. OPPIE smiles and nods to the room. STRAUSS, front:)*

STRAUSS. I'll get that Jew commie if it's the last thing I do.

(Scene blackout. Glow on LILITH.)

LILITH. Ju-lius.

OPPIE. I thought you were gone.

LILITH *(shrugs)*. When you don't hear me anymore, then I'm gone.

OPPIE. I long for that day.

LILITH. The great silence? It will come soon enough.
    You'll miss my breath in your ear. As you will miss this Prestige.
    This grand role in the International Theater of War.

TELLER. Opje, what is the meaning—
    my funding is held up. Now that you have spoken to the committee.
    The top men say Yes, we come work on the Super. They call you first, and they don't want to work anymore. Why?

OPPIE. Those men made their own decisions.

TELLER. NO. YOU MADE THE DECISION.

OPPIE. If a man asks my opinion, I give it.

TELLER. Your opinion. Is wrong.
    And you are killing me, holding up this funding.

OPPIE. I cannot in good conscience counsel the government to spend billions on a project unlikely to produce practical results.

TELLER. You will kill us all. *(He stalks off.)*

LILITH. The man with the Atomic Answers, molding public policy.

OPPIE. It's a matter of where one is called—

LILITH. Personal scientific advisor to the President.

OPPIE. someone had to—

LILITH. Cover of Life magazine. Interviews on television. Rushing Einstein for the title of most famous theoretical physicist in the world!

OPPIE. I didn't seek—all this. Before the war theoretical physics was among the most esoteric of all academic disciplines, comparable to Medieval French Poetry or… Sanskrit. Akin, almost, to taking the cloth.

But this is not angels dancing on the head of a pin
this is splitting the smallest increment of the head of the pin releasing
the Fury inside
the Fury at this
violation.
or we were the angels
dancing on the head of that pin
that pin that was about to
explode

LILITH. boom.

OPPIE. I did not court this. Fame. I did not seek it out.

LILITH. But you liked it.

OPPIE. I have never claimed to be super-human. I liked it, yes.

LILITH. Yessssssss.

OPPIE. And I had a responsibility. Someone had to tell them. We must not go on from here. There is no need for a bomb, fifty, a hundred times the power of the one that leveled Hiroshima.

RABI. But how can we be sure the Russians aren't working towards one?

That plan of Teller's, with the addition by Fuchs, could perhaps be workable.

OPPIE. A nuclear explosion as ignition? It will blow itself apart long before the thermo-nuclear reaction is triggered.

And besides, Russia suffered greatly in this war. They need to rebuild first. The only way Stalin could be devoting significant resources to an atomic program would be to starve his people.

RABI. You're right. Only a madman would—

LILITH. And so it was that a madman starved his people to create the magnificent explosion. Left Siberia without electricity so that a handful of young scientists would never be without what they needed to make the big explosion.

and then

THE BRITISH ENVOY

BRITISH ENVOY. Beg your pardon, so sorry to trouble you. But it looks as if we're in a bit of a rough spot, something of a sticky wicket, so to speak.

Chocolate? So nice not to have it rationed anymore, what?

Ahem. It seems our intelligence has uncovered something of a Spy Ring at your Los Alamos, there. Chap by the name of Greenglass, Jewish fellow, seems his contact was Harry Gold, another, well you know. Transmitted the information through a Julius *Rosenberg*. Greenglass' brother-in-law. Keep it in the family, eh?

Apparently they're all very gung-ho about this classless society for the worker business—

Toffee? They're rather good.

Er, ahem. How did we find all this out? Well, it's a funny story. It's through the...eh...the fellow we sent you. Klaus Fuchs.

Funny little chap. Glasses.

Yes. It seems he's a Russian Agent.

So sorry, but you know we were a trifle busy, what with the V2's raining down. Perhaps if our allies had been a little quicker to enter the war, there'd have been more time for the paperwork, what?

Turkish Delight?

(At the mentions of the name, LILITH sings an echo: "Green glass. Greenglass." TELLER strides on, shoving a large sheaf of papers into OPPIE's hands.)

TELLER. Fuchs was there. In the room. HE WAS IN CHARGE OF WRITING UP ALL THE NOTES. A spy! A damned spy among us! Sending all my ideas straight to MOTHER RUSSIA. They stole my country when I was a boy, and now they will STEAL THE VERY IDEAS FROM MY MIND. Fuchs thinks there is possibility to succeed. Ah? And so do the Russians. I need MONEY. I need MEN. a CRASH PROGRAM. NOW. We MUST HAVE THE SUPER.

(Under TELLER's rant, OPPIE has been looking at his papers, frowning. Gradually, his face relaxes, then breaks into a soft smile.)

OPPIE *(muttering)*. X-rays. Trigger the thermonuclear reaction almost instantaneously using x-rays.

LILITH. And you said it was

OPPIE. Sweet.

LILITH. Sssssssweeeeeeet.

OPPIE. This...this could work.

TELLER. *What?* You now...*yes?*
and what of your precious Scruples? Mmmm?

OPPIE. When you see something that is technically sweet, you go ahead and do it and argue about what to do about it only after you have had your technical success.

LILITH. And what *of* your precious scruples?

OPPIE *(looks at her)*. The calculations... It was...beautiful.

TELLER. So you will return then to Los Alamos? *(Beat.)*

OPPIE. No.
This one's yours. *(TELLER bows curtly, exits.)*

LILITH. If a thing is beautiful, it should go on? No matter what the consequences?

OPPIE. It's hard to think of consequences.
When a thing is so beautiful.

LILITH. Ah yes.
And the island of Elugelab disappeared beneath the sea.
To protect against the Communist Menace.
Embodied for the country as a little Jewish couple from the Lower East Side.
oh the terror you could inspire with that word
Rosenberg.

ETHEL

LILITH. Ethel ethel ethel. Ethel didn't know what hit her. Home making latkes. Noodle Kugel. Didn't know U-235 from Saltpeter. Didn't didn't didn't. Didn't know what hitler.

Except in her blood. Ethel ethel ethel. Her blood remembers the shtetl. Her blood sings *(She sings softly.)*
Ethel.
The cossacks have come again.

As the gas flows like liquid into her lungs.
They didn't pull her teeth.

The government of the United States of America does not melt down the gold from the teeth of the Jews it gasses.

OPPIE. She was electrocuted.

LILITH. Mmmmm. All the difference.

oppie oppie oppie. So ethical. So cultural.
What do you do when they point the finger at you and say
HE'S POISONED THE WELL AGAIN.

STRAUSS GETS THE CALL

(Ringing. STRAUSS, wearing a yarmulke, picks up an enormous phone.)

STRAUSS. Yes?
Yes, Mr. President.
Head of the Atomic Energy Commission?

Yes, sir!
Thank you, sir!
(Hangs up phone, clenching the yarmulke in one fist.)

I'll get that Jew commie if it's the last thing I do! *(Proclaims grandly.)* Bring me the head of J. Robert Oppenheimer.

J. EDGAR HOOVER DOES THE DANCE OF THE SEVEN VEILS

(Music: Salome. Light rises on J. EDGAR HOOVER, his back to the audience, swathed in long scarves. He does the dance of the seven veils, removing one for each charge read. In the end, he is revealed in a sober gray suit and tie.)

STRAUSS. Mr. Hoover, I have here a letter I think you will find of interest…

I will read only the salient parts…

the subject is J. Robert Oppenheimer. In the pre-war period, there is evidence that Oppenheimer

1. Contributed substantial monthly sums to the Communist Party.

2. Had, and still has, a wife and a brother who are Communists.

3. Had at least one Communist Mistress.

During the war, there is evidence that:

4. He was responsible for employing a number of communists at Los Alamos

5. He was a vigorous supporter of the H-bomb program until Hiroshima, Aug. 6, 1945, on which day he personally urged each senior individual working in this field to desist and

6. He was an enthusiastic sponsor of the A-bomb until the war ended, when he immediately and outspokenly advocated that the Los Alamos laboratory be disbanded.

After the war, Oppenheimer:
7. Worked tirelessly to retard the H-bomb program.

In conclusion, we must realize that

STRAUSS & HOOVER. More probably than not, Dr. Oppenheimer is an espionage agent under Soviet Direction.

HOOVER. Erect a Blank Wall between this man and any top-secret documents currently in his purview. Confiscate his filing cabinets. And subpoena that mistress!

STRAUSS. We can't, sir. She's dead.

HOOVER. A dead red?

STRAUSS. Yes, sir.

HOOVER *(sighs)*. I never thought I'd be sorry to hear those words.

OPPIE. Are they talking about Jean?

LILITH. Of course.

OPPIE. Mistress. That's ridiculous.

LILITH. Did you sleep with her?

OPPIE. Yes.

(JEAN appears in back, dancing vaguely to the same waltz.)

LILITH. When you were not married?

OPPIE. Yes.

I considered us engaged, but she never—

LILITH. And also, when you were married. To someone else.

OPPIE. yes.

LILITH. Then what was she, if not your mistress?

OPPIE. She was...a friend.

LILITH. a friend.

  With black hair. And green eyes.

OPPIE. yes

LILITH. and immaculate breeding.

OPPIE. soft cool hands, touching my face.

  as if— *(JEAN disappears.)*

LILITH. Were you a disappointment to her?

OPPIE. Jean?

LILITH *(cocks an eyebrow)*. Your mother.

OPPIE. Why?

LILITH. Because you weren't Normal.

OPPIE *(smiling)*. I suppose I wasn't, at that.

  Gave my first lecture to the New York Mineralogical Society at twelve. They didn't know I was twelve until I got there. I had submitted a paper, which they asked me to read.

  I suppose my parents were a bit...worried. They tried sending me to camp, the next year, but the other boys locked me in an icehouse overnight.

LILITH. Because you were Jewish?

OPPIE *(laughs)*. It was a Jewish camp.

  Because I was an insufferable little prick, I suppose.

LILITH. And were you a disappointment to Jean?

OPPIE. Oh, yes. I, and the world.

  Very much.

LILITH. And in the end, a disappointment to your Government.

  Because the Government has ideas about creation, too. Took it upon themselves to create a Scientific Advisor. And he may be a Jew, but he's from this country.

Speaks without an accent! And he's tall and elegant and cultured. A wise man, a pretty man. And he makes the bomb that ends the war. A tall bringer of miracles. He unleashes the power inside the tiny things you can't see. These Atoms.

But then he throws his intellect around like a Lariat, knocking things off the shelves. And he tells everyone the Hydrogen Bomb will be bad.

Then you have to throw him out.
get yourself a new one who will
LIE DOWN.

HEARING

(STRAUSS bangs a large gavel.)

STRAUSS. Dr. Oppenheimer, you realize this is not a trial. *(Smiles a big smile.)* This is merely a hearing to determine whether your security clearance will be renewed.

OPPIE. I do not believe that there are any new charges against me. I believe these are the same issues that did not stand in the way of my being granted clearance in wartime.

LILITH. when they needed you.

STRAUSS. This is a proceeding in which classified material will be discussed. In the interest of National Security, during such discussions your lawyers, who do not have clearance, will have to leave the room.

LILITH. Sssssecurity.

(Throughout the following, STRAUSS' monologue is continuous, leaping into the foreground where noted.)

TOWER OF BABEL

OPPIE. Security would have had us all Separate. Isolated. Ignorant. Speaking different languages. But I changed all that. I said
build us a great rabbit-warren. Our minds will breed. Lock out the world. Lock us in. Together.
And they argued, all those bright bright minds.
Would have been speaking different languages. If not for me. But I listened and I smoothed and I interpreted and I moved on to the next conflict and we
kept building
I made an Orchestra and we
kept building
And we reached God.
And he vaporized the tower. Fused the sand below into beautiful green glass that set the geiger counters clicking like locusts in the desert.

STRAUSS. And also that you caused to be hired various communists, and in fact ONLY communists, to work at Los Alamos.
Rossi Lomanitz
Joseph Weinberg
David Bohm
Max Friedman—
That a number of graduate students in Dr. Oppenheimer's "inner circle" at Berkeley were either Communists or "fellow travelers"—

OPPIE. Is this the part where you peck out my liver?

LILITH. Pro-me-te-O—!

Don't use references the committee won't get. Only makes them ANGRY.

STRAUSS. That in fact his own Brother was a card-carrying member of the Communist Party prior to his employment at the top-secret Los Alamos labs—

OPPIE. All that time. All that money. My god, we could have built another bomb with the money spent surveilling me.

And still. Those secrets walked themselves out.

Because secrets have no place in Science.

And Science has no place in War.

LILITH. Science has always been about war.

OPPIE. That's not true.

LILITH. Metallurgy was invented for spearheads, not plowshares.

Discovery is always about getting the one-up on the next guy.

Bigger club. Bigger bomb.

OPPIE. Science is about the free flow of ideas. It knows no borders. It is a* community of *minds*.

LILITH *(overlapping)*. *A community of minds that needs the Army to foot the bills. Pay for the philosophers' keep. And their cyclotrons.

OPPIE. Fuchs didn't…*steal* these ideas, he *had* them.

Why, he proposed the alteration to Teller's Super that made the damned thing workable.

LILITH. You make a bargain with the devil, he's going to come one day and want your soul. He will organize a committee to get it. Have himself a Hearing.

JEAN

STRAUSS. That on June 12, 1943, he was followed to the rooms of a known Communist woman, Jean Tatlock. He did not see fit to inform security, either before or after this incident—

(OPPIE hears these words with a certain shock. Breathes for a moment.)

OPPIE. Surveilled and surveilled and surveilled.
Wartime and beyond.
WHAT IS THIS, RUSSIA?
The last night I spent with a woman who felt Death breathing down her back. That last night Violated. As they watched the house. Or had it Bugged.
Our last sad…love.
There were tears involved, if I recall correctly. all these years later.

I recall correctly.
I recall…everything.
Blue veins across her white skin.
Freckles on her shoulders from the sun.
The curve of her back as she…bent to unbuckle a shoe.
Those eyes.
That I had…got lost in. Many a time.
Now *she* was lost in them.
Staring out of her face at me, as if
as if I possessed some sort of Answer and when I did-n't…

I, who was now no longer lost in the unswimmable
green depths of her eyes but Found
in the yellow sand of Los Alamos.

I saw her there, receding from the world.
like a ghost

(JEAN appears, wearing a long silk robe.)

But I was of the world now, in the world and I had to
serve it. To save it. Not her. Anymore.

Just this one night to hold her thin shaking body in my
arms.
As they waked and watched from their cars outside.

No, the security men must not have bugged the house.
Or they would know
We did not speak of Communism that night.

*(JEAN opens her robe. She wears a petal-pink silk slip.
Burns on her body, in the shape of flowers. She opens
her mouth—red, yellow, orange petals like flame.)*

Make it stop.
  please make it stop *(LILITH clicks at him.)*
STRAUSS. We will now hear testimony from Isador Rabi.
  Top-secret matters may be referred to, so would Dr.
  Oppenheimer's legal team kindly leave the room.
LILITH. as Kitty smokes in the corridor outside

(STRAUSS monologue out.)

KITTY SMOKES IN THE CORRIDOR OUTSIDE

KITTY. Bastards.
  Bastards.
  Bastards.

  D'you hear that, Joe Dallet? You and your god-damned
  Party. Your sleek, incomparable Ideals. And I fell for
  you. In my bright party dress. And then there were no
  more party dresses, just the Party. Hardly any dresses at
  all. Left behind comfort and ease, and that vague sense
  of unease that comes with. Left behind my family's
  money, as you had. Fighting for the Worker. Fighting
  against your Father and his fat money, money made
  striding over the backs of the poor. I fell for you and
  your sweet rightness, and love was enough for anything.
  Married in a plain blue dress at City Hall, and love was
  enough for anything. Living in a one-room flat with ten-
  ement heat and five-cent meals in the greasy restaurant
  downstairs, because the stove leaked and might blow us
  all up. And love was not enough, Joe. I missed hot water, and pretty clothes, and steak. And college. So I went
  back. Sat in that big living room in my pretty dress and
  the unease settling like an angry saint on my shoulders.
  Didn't know Mother was intercepting your letters. I
  thought you were disgusted with my weakness. Finally I
  broke, wrote begging you to take me back. By then you
  were fighting fascists in Spain. Said you'd never stopped
  loving me a day. We were to meet in Paris but instead I
  got the telegram. And the official condolences of the
  god-damned Party. *(Smokes.)*
  A dead man is no good to me, Joe.

Pretty speeches and pretty ideals. You bled to death on a field in Spain.

Stalin did not feed his people. There is no free state for the worker.

A dead man is no good to me, Joe. I'll take a gin martini any day. And the love of a man who is here. With his arms around me. At the head of our table, with our children. Leaning down to kiss the top of my hair.

You'd like him, Joe. You'd say he's good for me.

You hear that? In there?
They're killing him.
This will kill him.

Right now they're asking about his wife and her Party Membership.

If he muttered Atomic Secrets in his sleep, would I pass them along to Mother Russia. *(Smokes.)*

Mother Russia. If I ever see the old bitch I'll scratch her eyes out.

Tell her to stop killing
my men.

RABI AND TELLER

LILITH. And Rabi says

RABI. This is simply ridiculous. All during Los Alamos and after, you have had men following my good friend, Dr. Oppenheimer. Don't you think if there *was* anything, you'd have found it?

Here you have a guy who is a consultant. If you don't like the advice he gives, don't consult him. Period.

Above all, the man's contribution to this country must be weighed.
There is a real, positive record... We have an H-bomb and a whole series of them. What more do you want, mermaids?

LILITH. And Teller says

TELLER. I know Oppenheimer as an intellectually most alert and very complicated person, and I think it would be presumptuous and wrong on my part if I would try in any way to analyze his motives.

STRAUSS. Do you or do you not believe that Dr Oppenheimer is a security risk?

TELLER. I believe that Dr. Oppenheimer's character is such that he would not knowingly and wittingly do anything that is designed to endanger the safety of this country. To the extent, therefore, that your question is directed toward intent, I would say I do not see any reason to deny clearance. If it is a question of wisdom and judgement, as demonstrated by actions since 1945, then I would say one would be wiser not to grant clearance.

LILITH. Sssssssooooo Teller comes back to haunt you. Because you turned your back on his big beautiful explosion.

OPPIE. We had done calculations, but none of us really understood... The photos* came back from Hiroshima—

LILITH *(*overlapping)*. The dead of Hiroshima are NOTHING. I have seen Hisssssstory. People fall. You blink and a thousand lie at your feet. They become dirt.

Again. Return to that black muck that God shaped me out of. But you—

OPPIE. There was a woman missing three fingers* from her right hand.

LILITH. *I have seen thousands. Hundred thousands. I saw your mother birth you. I should have taken you then. red and squalling but something told me no. this one will be interesssssssting. this one will not LIE DOWN. for another century. Thisssssss one will take the rage of the Jews and make it explode.

OPPIE *(soft)*. I wanted to know…how the world worked.

LILITH. You wanted to KILL.

OPPIE. No.

LILITH. You could have voted for a demonstration.

OPPIE. They wouldn't have gone* for a demonstration…

LILITH. *No.

But you could have voted for one.

You suggested Hiroshima.

OPPIE. We gave them a list…

LILITH. You suggested Nagasaki

OPPIE. of possible targets that would appropriately demonstrate the

OPPIE & LILITH. destructive force *(OPPIE coughs. Lights another cigarette.)*

LILITH. And then you turned your back.

On that sheer beautiful destructive force.

Teller could see in his mind's eye. The bomb ignited by the bomb. Atomic blast captured and held. Until fusion the great destructive force that fuels the sun

until fusion happened.

and then it would not be the hundred-foot tower you'd built to hold the bomb vaporized, as at your pretty Trinity. But the whole island it was sitting on. A mile-wide crater in the ocean floor.

HOW BEAUTIFUL
You turned your back on the thing you made happen.

God breathed into my mouth
but he sided with the other one
split him open and took out a rib

I spoke the sacred name of God and I
exploded
with a light as bright as a thousand suns.

CLEARANCE REVOKED

STRAUSS. It is the decision of this Board that the clearance of J. Robert Oppenheimer shall not be renewed.
LILITH. And now you know.
    What it is to be cast out.

    you will be an old man.
    wandering the desert
    without the company of your own kind
    without the company of your
    creation.

    (Silence. The desert again. OPPIE is alone.)

OPPIE. At least it's quiet. *(He coughs delicately.)*
    At least I'm at Princeton. *(He coughs again, spits into a handkerchief.)*

Beneath the pretty trees. *(Silence.)*
But I am forbidden to touch
to teach
to hear
to know

the discipline grows, changes
and I
am on the outside.
Forbidden to enter
the room.

(A silence. JEAN appears. Smoking.)

VOICEOVER. Dr. Oppenheimer? It's time for your test.

JEAN. You don't do a woman any favors, putting her on a pedestal. Just another way to avoid looking her in the eye.

OPPIE *(looks at JEAN)*. Jean—
I'm sorry, I—

JEAN *(touches his face)*. Shhhh. *(Smoke rises behind OPPIE's head.)*
you've got to be still while they take the picture.

(Sound of an x-ray. JEAN is gone. Silence. OPPIE looks for LILITH, but she is nowhere.)

CANCER

VOICEOVER (INTERVIEWER). Dr. Oppenheimer?
(OPPIE looks toward the voice.)

Dr. Oppenheimer, can you tell us what your first thoughts were upon seeing the explosion at Trinity?

OPPIE *(tired. He's said this before)*. A line from the Bhagavad-Gita crossed my mind. Krishna assumes his powerful, many-armed form and he says

Now I am become Death, the destroyer of worlds.

VOICEOVER (INTERVIEWER). Dr. Oppenheimer, could you tell us what your thoughts are on what our Atomic Policy should be?

OPPIE. No, I can't do that. I'm not close enough to the facts. And I'm not close enough to the thoughts of those who are worrying about it.

LILITH. All thisssss...
    It *sticks in your throat*
    doesn't it?

OPPIE *(coughs, smiles at her return)*. Yes.

LILITH. Where it grows.
    taking on a life of its own.

OPPIE *(composing a letter)*. My Dear Hans. Thanks for your inquiries as to my health. My cancer is spreading rapidly; thus I am being radiated further, this time with electrons from a betatron.

(Pause. He laughs. pause. KITTY is watching him from the doorway.)

LILITH. If you do something beautifully, why stop?
    (OPPIE looks at LILITH.)
    The cancer is not thinking of the consequences. It is thinking only of blossoming. growing.

OPPIE. yes.

LILITH. exploding in your bloodstream. *(OPPIE smiles.)*

OPPIE. Kitty. Darling, please bring me a cigarette.

KITTY. The doctor says no cigarettes.

OPPIE. Kitty, please. Let's be objective. I am dying. Denying myself the pleasure of tobacco is not going to alter that fact. *(KITTY is already lighting two cigarettes. Passes him one.)* Thank you, darling.

KITTY. As if I could deny you anything.

OPPIE. Re-writing history already? You used to make a sport of it.

KITTY. Only when you deserved it.

OPPIE. No, less often than that, surely.

KITTY *(looks at him. This interchange is very gentle between them)*. Can you eat some soup?

OPPIE. Oh, I don't think so.

KITTY. Some lime ice, then?

OPPIE *(smiles)*. Thank you. That sounds lovely. *(She exits.)* I can't help thinking if I'd been able to love Jean the way I love Kitty. The way I have *learned* to see— the real woman standing before me. Not some…theoretical ideal. *(In the next room, the phone rings.)*

LILITH. She'd still be alive?

OPPIE. I don't know about that. I was going to say, she'd have married me.

KITTY *(enters)*. You'll never guess who just phoned. It's the Government, darling. Those fuckers want to give you a prize now.

OPPIE. Oh, all right. I suppose.

KITTY. All right?

OPPIE *(shrugs)*. All right. Will the President give it himself?

KITTY. I'll find out. *(She exits, returns.)*
  Yes.
OPPIE. Well then. He's a brave young man.
KITTY. As soon as he returns from a trip to Dallas.
  (LILITH snorts.)

THE DEVIL

OPPIE. There is a Zen parable.
  A man sees a devil in the market. The merchant says,
  this is an excellent devil, able to do anything you want.
  For only 20,000 yen, I will give him to you
  The man agreed
  I must warn you, said the merchant, this devil is no
  good.
  —But you said he was an excellent devil
  That's true, the merchant said, but he will always remain
  a devil. You have to keep him busy every minute. If he
  has free time, if he doesn't know what to do, then he is
  dangerous.
  Well if that's all, said the man, and he took the devil
  home.

  It went very well.
  Each morning, the devil would kneel obediently while
  the man mapped out his chores for the day. Chop wood,
  light the stove, prepare my food, clean the house. All
  day the devil completed his tasks, at night he slept in his
  bamboo cage. It went on this way for months.
  Then one day the man ran into an old friend in town,
  and they got to drinking sake, one little stone jar after
  another, and they ended up in the willow quarter. The

ladies kept the two friends busy, and the next morning the man woke alone in a strange room. He paid the bill to the women, who looked quite different from what he remembered the previous evening, and hurried home.

From the road he saw smoke.

The devil had made an open fire, and was roasting the neighbor's child on a spit. *(Beat.)*

I thought we were cracking open the secrets of the universe.

LILITH. You were.

OPPIE. I thought it would be a geode.

Shining in the first light of discovery.

LILITH. It is a geode filled with blood.

OPPIE. For only two billion dollars of the Army's money.

I will give him to you.

I have left a poisoned apple on the desk.

I must go back.

I must go back.

LILITH. There is no back.

Little man. But you know that.

OPPIE. *I should have been a pair of claws*
scuttling the ragged seas

LILITH. Shhh.

it's time.

OPPIE. Science was my passion. my path. my breath. my truest love.

LILITH. and because your love will not behave, does not balance statue-still on that pedestal but blows it to pieces, you turn your back on her? *(Beat.)*

OPPIE. No.

LILITH. No. Theory turns to practice.

OPPIE. The photos come back.

LILITH. The radioactivity lingers in half-lives of a billion years.

OPPIE. a lump grows in your throat

LILITH. And you go on.
Cursed and Blessed.

OPPIE *(smiles)*. I have heard the mermaids singing
in great howling sandstorms of desert winds and a fire-ball burst high above the earth.

For a full moment there was just the unbearable brightness. As the sound raced across the desert to catch up.

(LILITH waits.)

For a moment, in utter silence.
It had the light
of a thousand suns.

(Bright

dark

noise

curtain.)

END OF PLAY